SECRET OF INNER COMPASS

NAVIGATING LIFE WITH INTUITION

DR. MINAKSHI BANSAL

Made with ♥ on the Notion Press Platform
www.notionpress.com

DEDICATION

To all the seekers, dreamers, and wanderers, who dare to trust their inner compass and chart their own unique path through life.

ᗘᗘᗘ

Contents

Contents

Contents

Prayer

"Om Bhadram Karnebhih Shrinuyama Devah

Bhadram Pashyemakshabhiryajatrah

Sthirairangais Tushtuvamsastanubhih

Vyashema Devahitam Yadayuh

Svasti Na Indro Vriddhashravah

Svasti Nah Pusha Vishwavedah

Svasti Nastarkshyo Arishtanemih

Svasti No Brihaspatir Dadhatu

Om Shantih Shantih Shantih"

This mantra is a prayer for universal well-being, invoking the blessings of various deities for protection, health, and happiness. It emphasizes the importance of experiencing the auspicious through all senses and living a life aligned with divine purpose. The repetition of "Shantih" at the end signifies a deep desire for peace in the individual, the environment, and the universe at large. This mantra is often recited as a prayer for peace, prosperity, and the physical and spiritual well-being of all beings.

About The Author

This book represents the culmination of extensive research and meticulous analysis, incorporating a diverse range of sources, including numerous books, scholarly studies, and personal experiences. Additionally, I have scoured various websites to gather relevant information and data essential for the compilation of this work. I have taken every precaution to ensure the accuracy of the information presented and have diligently cited all sources to acknowledge their contributions.

From her earliest days, Minakshi was distinguished by an insatiable appetite for reading. Her literary universe was inhabited by characters and narratives that spanned ethical tales, motivational and inspirational stories, and the mythic parables imbued with life lessons. This voracious reading habit was not merely for personal edification but was driven by a desire to distill and disseminate the essence of these narratives to foster the development of students and peers alike. She was particularly captivated by the lives and teachings of historical figures and spiritual leaders such as Adi Shankaracharya, Swami Vivekananda, Dr. APJ Abdul Kalam, Mahamana Pandit Madan Mohan Malviya, Mahatma Gandhi, Sardar Vallabhai Patel, and Vinoba Bhave, among others. Their philosophies and life stories fueled her ambition to embody their ideals of resilience, selflessness, and relentless pursuit of knowledge.

Dr. Minakshi's academic and practical engagement with psychology has been equally noteworthy. As a research scholar, her focus has been on exploring the intricate tapestry of the human psyche, aiming to unlock the potential for psychological well-being and societal harmony. Her scholarly work is complemented by her active involvement in social work, where she employs her academic insights to make tangible differences in the lives of the underprivileged. Her endeavours in social work are characterized by an innovative approach that combines traditional wisdom with contemporary psychological practices to address the multifaceted challenges faced by these communities.

Her artistic talents, another facet of her diverse capabilities, are not merely a personal passion but also serve as a medium through which she communicates and connects with others. Her art, rich in symbolism and emotional depth, reflects her philosophical inquiries and social concerns, offering viewers a glimpse into the breadth of her intellect and the depth of her compassion.

In addition to her contributions to the arts and social sciences, Dr. Minakshi has embraced the healing arts of Pranic Healing, mastering the techniques developed by Master Choa Kok Sui. This practice, which focuses on the manipulation of Prana or life energy to heal the body and aura, has been both a personal journey of discovery and a means through which she extends her healing touch to others. Her proficiency in Pranic Healing is complemented by her advocacy and teaching of various forms of meditation aimed at rejuvenation, personal betterment, and the cultivation of harmony within individuals and communities alike.

Dr. Minakshi's life is a narrative of relentless pursuit, not just of personal achievement but of the upliftment and empowerment of society at large. Her diverse interests and talents—spanning the arts, literature, psychology, and the healing practices—converge on a singular path of service. She embodies the spirit of the luminaries who inspired her, channelling their legacy through her actions and teachings. Through her books, art, and social initiatives, she continues to inspire a new generation to embark on their own journeys of self-discovery, resilience, and altruism.

Her commitment to social betterment, particularly her focus on uplifting underprivileged children, reflects a deep understanding of the transformative potential of education and personal development. By integrating her knowledge of psychology, her artistic sensibilities, and her healing practices, Dr. Bansal has developed a holistic approach to social work that addresses both the immediate needs and the long-term well-being of the communities she serves.

As an author, Dr. Minakshi's writings offer a blend of inspirational insights, practical wisdom, and reflective contemplations drawn from her extensive reading and life experiences. Her books serve as a guide for those seeking to navigate the complexities of life with grace, resilience, and purpose. Through her narratives, she extends an invitation to her readers to explore the depths of their own potential and to contribute meaningfully to the collective well-being of society.

In Dr. Minakshi Bansal, we find a remarkable synthesis of the artist, the scholar, the healer, and the social activist. Her life's work stands as a beacon of hope and a source of inspiration for individuals seeking to make a difference in the world. Her story is a compelling reminder of the power of individual action, rooted in compassion and driven by a profound commitment to the betterment of humanity. Dr. Minakshi's legacy is not just in the tangible outcomes of her efforts but in the enduring spirit of inquiry, empathy, and service that she embodies.

ppp

Preface

In the tapestry of life, woven with threads of joy, sorrow, triumph, and adversity, we all yearn for a guiding light, a compass that can lead us through the labyrinthine pathways of our existence. While logic and reason serve as invaluable tools for navigating the external world, there is another, more subtle force at play—a quiet whisper within, a gut feeling, an intuitive nudge that can lead us towards our truest selves and most fulfilling destinies.

This book is an invitation to embark on a journey of self-discovery, to reconnect with the innate wisdom that resides within each of us. It is a celebration of intuition, that often-overlooked faculty that can guide us towards greater clarity, confidence, and authenticity in every aspect of our lives. Through personal anecdotes, practical exercises, and insightful reflections, I will share with you the tools and techniques I have discovered for harnessing the power of intuition and navigating life with grace, courage, and purpose.

My own journey with intuition has been a lifelong exploration, marked by moments of profound insight, exhilarating breakthroughs, and humbling setbacks. I have learned that intuition is not a mystical power reserved for the chosen few, but a universal gift that can be cultivated and strengthened through practice and self-awareness. It is a skill that can be honed, a muscle that can be flexed, and a compass that can be calibrated to guide us towards our truest north.

In the pages that follow, we will delve into the many facets of intuition, exploring its origins, its manifestations, and its applications in various areas of our lives. We will discuss how to quiet the mind, cultivate mindfulness, and create space for our intuition to emerge. We will explore the power of nature, creativity, and dreams as conduits for intuitive guidance. We will also delve into the challenges and obstacles that can hinder our intuition, offering practical strategies for overcoming them.

Through personal anecdotes and real-life examples, I will share the transformative power of intuition in my own life and the lives of countless others. We will see how intuition can guide us towards fulfilling careers, meaningful relationships, and authentic self-expression. We will also explore how intuition can help us navigate through difficult times, providing comfort, clarity, and direction when we need it most.

This book is not a prescriptive guide, but rather an invitation to embark on your own unique journey of intuitive discovery. There is no one-size-fits-all approach to intuition, as each of us has our own unique way of receiving and interpreting intuitive guidance. My hope is that this book will serve as a catalyst for your own exploration, inspiring you to trust your inner wisdom and embrace the power of intuition in your life.

Whether you are a seasoned intuitive or just beginning to explore this fascinating realm, I believe that this book has something to offer you. It is my heartfelt wish that it will empower you to tap into your own innate wisdom, navigate life's challenges with grace and confidence, and create a life that is aligned with your deepest values and aspirations.

May this book be a beacon of light on your journey, illuminating the path towards a more intuitive, authentic, and fulfilling life.

Dr. Minakshi Bansal
Social Activist
Ahmedabad, Gujarat, Bharat

ONE

THE WHISPER WITHIN: INTRODUCING THE CONCEPT OF INTUITION AS AN INNER GUIDE

Have you ever experienced a sudden flash of insight, a gut feeling that told you to do something or avoid a certain path? That inexplicable nudge, that whisper within, is intuition, your inner compass guiding you through life's labyrinthine pathways. It's a sense of knowing that transcends logic and reason, a subtle yet powerful force that can lead you to unexpected discoveries and profound truths.

Intuition is not a mystical power reserved for the chosen few; it is a universal gift, an inherent aspect of our human experience. Think of it as a wise friend residing deep within your soul, a silent advisor who understands your desires, fears, and dreams better than anyone else. It speaks a language that transcends words, communicating through subtle feelings, images, and sensations.

Your intuition is not separate from you; it is an integral part of your being, a reflection of your innermost self. It draws upon the vast reservoir of your life experiences, knowledge, and subconscious wisdom. It processes information beyond the reach of your conscious mind, synthesizing it into a holistic understanding that often defies explanation.

The whisper within can manifest in various ways. It might be a gentle tugging in your heart, a tingling sensation in your gut, a sudden clarity of thought, or a flash of inspiration. It can emerge as a hunch, a knowingness, or a deep-seated conviction. It might even appear in your dreams, offering symbolic messages and guidance.

Learning to recognize and trust your intuition is a transformative journey. It requires quieting the external noise and distractions, creating space for the whispers within to emerge. It involves cultivating a receptive and open-minded attitude, embracing the unknown with curiosity and wonder.

Intuition is not a substitute for rational thinking; rather, it complements and enhances it. It offers a different perspective, a holistic understanding that takes into account factors beyond the realm of logic. By integrating intuition into your decision-making process, you tap into a deeper level of wisdom and insight.

Embracing your intuition allows you to connect with your authentic self, your true desires, and your purpose in life. It helps you navigate challenges with greater clarity and resilience, make choices that align with your values, and cultivate more meaningful relationships. It empowers you to live a life that is true to your heart, a life filled with passion, purpose, and joy.

Throughout history, countless individuals have attributed their success and breakthroughs to their intuition. Scientists, artists, entrepreneurs, and spiritual leaders have all spoken about the importance of trusting their inner voice. They recognized that intuition is not a random occurrence, but a reliable source of guidance that can lead them to extraordinary achievements.

The journey of cultivating your intuition is a lifelong adventure. It is a process of self-discovery, of learning to listen to your inner wisdom with ever-increasing clarity and confidence. It is about embracing your intuition as a trusted companion, a guide who can lead you to a life filled with meaning, purpose, and fulfillment.

In the following chapters, we will explore the nature of intuition, its various forms, and the ways in which you can cultivate and strengthen your connection to your inner compass. We will delve into practical techniques for accessing your intuition, overcoming common obstacles, and integrating intuitive guidance into your daily life. We will also discuss the role of intuition in personal growth, decision-making, relationships, creativity, and spirituality.

Remember, your intuition is a unique and personal gift. There is no right or wrong way to experience it. Trust your own inner wisdom, listen to the whispers within, and allow your intuition to guide you on your path.

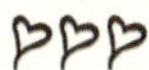

Intuition is the whisper of your soul, a gentle nudge guiding you towards your true path. It speaks a language beyond words, a feeling of resonance that transcends logic and reason. Listen closely, for its wisdom holds the key to your highest potential.

TWO

BEYOND LOGIC: EXPLORING THE DIFFERENCE BETWEEN INTUITIVE AND RATIONAL THINKING

While logic serves as our intellectual scaffolding, intuition often acts as the hidden architect, influencing our decisions and perceptions in profound ways. Understanding the distinction between intuitive and rational thinking can unlock a treasure trove of self-awareness and empower us to navigate life's complexities with greater wisdom and clarity.

Rational thinking, often celebrated as the cornerstone of modern society, is a methodical process rooted in analysis, reasoning, and evidence. It relies on objective data, cause-and-effect relationships, and step-by-step deductions to arrive at conclusions. It is the language of science, mathematics, and engineering, the domain of facts, figures, and empirical observations.

Intuition, on the other hand, operates in a realm beyond logic's reach. It is a subjective experience, a felt sense of knowing that arises spontaneously, often without conscious deliberation. It is the voice of our subconscious mind, drawing upon a vast reservoir of accumulated experiences, tacit knowledge, and emotional intelligence.

While logic excels at dissecting problems into manageable components and evaluating them systematically, intuition grasps the whole picture effortlessly. It connects disparate dots, revealing hidden patterns and underlying connections that elude the linear processes of rational thought.

Logic thrives on tangible evidence and verifiable facts, while intuition dances with hunches, gut feelings, and inexplicable insights. It is the whisper in the wind, the fleeting shadow that catches our peripheral vision, the sudden flash of understanding that illuminates a previously murky path.

Logic is often slow and deliberate, carefully weighing each option before reaching a conclusion. Intuition, on the other hand, can be swift and spontaneous, offering guidance in the blink of an eye. It is the instinct that prompts us to swerve our car to avoid an accident, the intuitive leap that leads a scientist to a groundbreaking discovery.

While logic prides itself on its objectivity, intuition is inherently subjective, colored by our unique perspectives, values, and emotions. It is the filter through which we interpret the world, shaping our perceptions, biases, and beliefs.

Logic seeks certainty and predictability, striving to eliminate ambiguity and uncertainty. Intuition embraces the unknown, navigating the gray areas of life with grace and agility. It thrives in the realms of creativity, art, and spirituality, where ambiguity and open-endedness are not obstacles but catalysts for growth and exploration.

The interplay between intuitive and rational thinking is a delicate dance, a constant negotiation between head and heart. Logic provides the structure, the framework within which intuition can flourish. Intuition, in turn, infuses logic with a sense of meaning, purpose, and direction.

By embracing both modes of thinking, we unlock the full potential of our cognitive faculties. We can leverage logic's rigor and precision to analyze complex problems, while drawing upon intuition's wisdom and insight to navigate the uncharted territories of life.

In the realm of personal relationships, intuition can guide us towards deeper connections and greater understanding. It helps us decipher nonverbal cues, sense unspoken emotions, and build trust based on gut feelings rather than mere appearances.

In the world of business, intuition can be a valuable asset, enabling entrepreneurs to identify opportunities, anticipate market trends, and make bold decisions that defy conventional wisdom. It is the spark that ignites innovation, the catalyst for disruptive change.

In the pursuit of personal growth, intuition can serve as a compass, guiding us towards our true passions and purpose in life. It helps us connect with our authentic selves, make choices that align with our values, and live a life that is both meaningful and fulfilling.

The journey towards integrating intuitive and rational thinking is a lifelong endeavor. It requires cultivating self-awareness, developing our emotional intelligence, and learning to trust our gut instincts. It involves recognizing the strengths and limitations of each mode of thinking, and finding a harmonious balance between them.

By embracing the synergy between logic and intuition, we can unlock a deeper understanding of ourselves, the world around us, and the infinite possibilities that lie beyond the confines of rational thought. We can tap into the wisdom of our hearts, the whispers of our souls, and navigate the complexities of life with grace, clarity, and purpose.

ppp

In the stillness of your being, the compass of your intuition awakens. It points not to external validation but to the uncharted territories of your heart's desires. Trust its guidance and embark on a journey of self-discovery.

THREE

A Universal Gift: How everyone possesses intuition, even if it's dormant

Intuition, often shrouded in mystery and misconstrued as a rare gift bestowed upon a select few, is in fact a universal human faculty, a dormant potential residing within each of us. It's the quiet hum of our subconscious mind, the subtle whispers of our inner wisdom, waiting to be awakened and embraced. Like a hidden talent or a buried treasure, intuition lies dormant within us, ready to be unearthed and harnessed for our personal growth and well-being.

The notion that intuition is an exclusive privilege is a misconception perpetuated by a culture that often prioritizes logic and reason over subjective experience. We are taught to rely on empirical evidence, concrete data, and rational analysis, while discounting the value of our gut feelings, hunches, and intuitive insights.

However, if we look beyond the surface of our conscious awareness, we discover a deeper level of knowing, a wellspring of wisdom that transcends the boundaries of logic and reason. This is the realm of intuition, the quiet voice that speaks to us through subtle signs, synchronicities, and seemingly inexplicable coincidences.

Intuition is not a supernatural power or a mystical ability, but rather an innate aspect of our human experience. It is the culmination of our life experiences, knowledge, and subconscious processing, a synthesis of information that goes beyond the limitations of our conscious mind.

Our intuition is constantly at work, even when we are not consciously aware of it. It guides our decisions, influences our perceptions, and shapes our interactions with the world around us. It is the force that attracts us to certain people, places, or opportunities, and repels us from others.

The dormancy of our intuition can be attributed to several factors. The fast-paced, information-saturated world we live in often leaves little room for quiet reflection and introspection. We are bombarded with stimuli from all directions, drowning out the subtle whispers of our inner voice.

Additionally, our upbringing and cultural conditioning may have taught us to distrust our intuition, labeling it as irrational or unreliable. We may have been told to ignore our gut feelings, to prioritize logic and reason over subjective experience.

Furthermore, fear and self-doubt can also block our intuitive channels. We may be afraid of making mistakes, of trusting our own judgment, or of being perceived as foolish or naive. These fears can stifle our intuition, preventing us from accessing its wisdom and guidance.

However, just as a neglected muscle can be strengthened through exercise, our dormant intuition can be awakened and cultivated through conscious effort and practice. By creating space for quiet reflection, engaging in mindfulness practices, and paying attention to our subtle feelings and sensations, we can begin to tap into the wisdom of our inner voice.

Connecting with nature, engaging in creative activities, and spending time in solitude can also help us access our intuition. By disconnecting from the external world and tuning in to our inner landscape, we create a fertile ground for intuitive insights to emerge.

Keeping a journal, documenting our dreams, and practicing divination techniques like tarot or oracle cards can also be helpful tools for exploring and developing our intuition. These practices can provide us with valuable insights into our subconscious mind, helping us to understand our deepest desires, fears, and motivations.

The journey of awakening our intuition is a personal one, unique to each individual. There is no one-size-fits-all approach, as our intuitive abilities manifest in different ways. Some people experience intuition as a gut feeling, others as a visual image or a symbolic message.

The key is to trust our own inner wisdom, to listen to the subtle whispers of our intuition, and to honor the messages it conveys. By embracing our intuition as a valuable guide, we can navigate life's challenges with greater clarity, confidence, and authenticity.

As we cultivate our intuition, we may find that it becomes more readily available and accessible to us. We may experience a greater sense of clarity, insight, and direction in our lives. We may also find that our intuition guides us towards greater fulfillment, joy, and purpose.

The awakening of our intuition is not a one-time event, but rather an ongoing process of self-discovery and personal growth. By nurturing our intuition, we tap into a wellspring of wisdom that can enrich our lives in countless ways.

ᐅᐅᐅ

Your intuition is not a fleeting emotion but a wellspring of ancient wisdom. It connects you to the collective consciousness, the universal truths that transcend time and space. Embrace its whispers, and you will find yourself in harmony with the universe.

FOUR

TRUSTING YOUR GUT: WHY THAT "GUT FEELING" IS OFTEN WORTH PAYING ATTENTION TO

The phrase "trust your gut" is more than a casual idiom; it's an acknowledgment of the profound wisdom residing within our bodies. That gnawing sensation in your stomach, the butterflies fluttering in your chest, or the subtle tightness in your throat - these are not mere physiological responses, but whispers from your intuition, your gut feeling, urging you to pay attention. Learning to trust these visceral signals can lead to a more authentic, fulfilling, and successful life.

Your gut feeling, often referred to as intuition, is a complex interplay of physiological responses, emotional cues, and subconscious processing. It's a culmination of your life experiences, knowledge, and instincts, seamlessly woven together to offer you guidance and direction. It's that nagging voice that tells you something isn't quite right, or the sudden surge of excitement that propels you towards a new opportunity.

Often dismissed as irrational or illogical, your gut feeling is, in fact, a highly sophisticated system of information processing. It taps into your vast reservoir of accumulated knowledge, analyzing and synthesizing it at a speed and depth that your conscious mind simply cannot match. It draws upon subtle cues from your environment, your interactions with others, and your own internal state, filtering and interpreting them to provide you with a holistic understanding of the situation at hand.

Your gut feeling is not infallible, of course. It can be influenced by your biases, fears, and past traumas. However, when cultivated and honed, it can become a reliable compass, guiding you towards decisions and actions that align with your true values and aspirations.

There are numerous reasons why trusting your gut feeling is often worth paying attention to. For one, it can help you make quick decisions in situations where time is of the essence. When faced with a complex problem or a pressing deadline, your gut feeling can cut through the clutter of information and offer a clear path forward.

Moreover, trusting your gut can lead you to opportunities that you might otherwise miss. It can nudge you towards taking risks, pursuing your passions, and stepping outside your comfort zone. By following your gut, you open yourself up to new experiences, new connections, and new possibilities.

Your gut feeling can also serve as a warning system, alerting you to potential dangers or pitfalls. It can signal when a person or situation is not to be trusted, or when a decision might not be in your best interest. By heeding these warning signs, you can avoid unnecessary heartache and setbacks.

Furthermore, trusting your gut can enhance your creativity and problem-solving abilities. It can lead you to innovative solutions and unconventional approaches that you might not have considered otherwise. By tapping into your intuition, you unlock a wellspring of creativity and insight.

Perhaps most importantly, trusting your gut can lead to a more authentic and fulfilling life. It can help you connect with your true desires, your passions, and your purpose. By following your gut, you make choices that are in alignment with your values and aspirations, leading to a life that is both meaningful and rewarding.

Of course, trusting your gut feeling is not always easy. It requires a willingness to let go of control, to embrace uncertainty, and to listen to the wisdom of your body and heart. It involves silencing the doubts and fears that can cloud your judgment, and cultivating a sense of trust in your own inner guidance.

There are various practices that can help you develop and strengthen your intuition. Meditation, mindfulness, and other forms of contemplative practice can create space for your gut feeling to emerge. Journaling, dream analysis, and creative expression can also provide valuable insights into your subconscious mind.

By learning to recognize and trust your gut feeling, you tap into a powerful source of wisdom and guidance. You gain access to a wealth of information that can help you make better decisions, navigate challenges with greater ease, and live a more authentic and fulfilling life. So, the next time you feel that tug in your gut, that subtle whisper of intuition, don't dismiss it. Pay attention, listen closely, and trust your gut. It might just lead you to a life you never imagined possible.

ᗡᗡᗡ

Nature, in its infinite wisdom, holds a mirror to your soul. It reflects your deepest emotions, desires, and fears. Wander amidst its beauty, and you will find your intuition awakened, guiding you towards clarity and peace.

FIVE

BODY WISDOM: HOW YOUR PHYSICAL SENSATIONS CAN OFFER INTUITIVE INSIGHTS

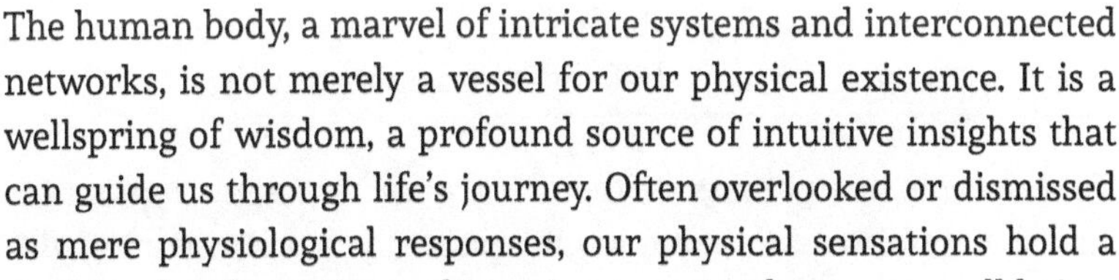

The human body, a marvel of intricate systems and interconnected networks, is not merely a vessel for our physical existence. It is a wellspring of wisdom, a profound source of intuitive insights that can guide us through life's journey. Often overlooked or dismissed as mere physiological responses, our physical sensations hold a wealth of information, whispering secrets about our well-being, emotions, and the world around us.

Our bodies are constantly communicating with us, sending subtle signals and nuanced cues that often go unnoticed in the hustle and bustle of daily life. A tightness in the chest, a knot in the stomach, a tingling sensation in the fingertips – these are not random occurrences, but messages from our subconscious mind, our intuition speaking through the language of the body.

This bodily wisdom, often referred to as somatic intelligence, is a form of embodied cognition, a deep knowing that resides within our cells and tissues. It is a primal form of communication, predating language and reason, that connects us to our instincts, emotions, and the world around us.

Our physical sensations are not separate from our thoughts and emotions; they are intimately intertwined, reflecting our inner state and providing valuable insights into our experiences. A racing heart may signal anxiety or excitement, while a relaxed body may indicate peace and contentment.

Our bodies also react to the energy of others, picking up on subtle cues and mirroring their emotions. A warm embrace can trigger a sense of comfort and belonging, while a cold stare can send shivers down our spine.

By paying attention to these subtle bodily cues, we can tap into a deeper level of awareness, a somatic intelligence that can guide us towards greater well-being and fulfillment. We can learn to decipher the messages our bodies are sending us, using them as a compass to navigate life's challenges and opportunities.

For example, a tightness in the chest may be a sign that we are holding onto stress or emotional pain. By acknowledging this sensation and exploring its origins, we can begin to release the pent-up energy and find a sense of peace and resolution.

A knot in the stomach may be a sign that we are feeling anxious or insecure about a particular situation. By tuning into this sensation and identifying its triggers, we can develop strategies for managing our anxiety and cultivating a greater sense of confidence and self-assurance.

A tingling sensation in the fingertips may be a sign that we are in the presence of something or someone that resonates with our energy. By paying attention to this sensation and exploring its significance, we can open ourselves up to new connections and experiences.

The language of the body is not always easy to decipher. It requires patience, self-awareness, and a willingness to explore the depths of our emotions and sensations. However, the rewards of developing this somatic intelligence are immeasurable.

By learning to trust our bodies and the wisdom they hold, we can make more informed decisions, cultivate healthier relationships, and live a more authentic and fulfilling life. We can tap into our intuition, our gut feelings, and the subtle cues that our bodies are constantly sending us.

There are various practices that can help us cultivate our somatic intelligence. Mindfulness meditation, yoga, and other forms of movement therapy can help us become more aware of our bodies and the sensations they experience. Body scan meditations, in particular, can be a powerful tool for cultivating this awareness.

Journaling, drawing, and other forms of creative expression can also help us connect with our bodies and express our emotions in a non-verbal way. By giving voice to our bodily wisdom, we can gain a deeper understanding of ourselves and the world around us.

Ultimately, cultivating somatic intelligence is a journey of self-discovery and self-acceptance. It is about learning to trust our bodies, to honor their wisdom, and to embrace the messages they are sending us. By doing so, we open ourselves up to a deeper level of knowing, a profound connection to our inner being, and a greater sense of peace, joy, and fulfillment in our lives.

ϷϷϷ

Art, music, and writing are not mere expressions of creativity; they are conduits for your intuition. Through these mediums, your soul speaks its truth, revealing hidden desires and untapped potential. Let your creativity flow, and your intuition will guide your hand.

SIX

QUIET THE MIND: MEDITATION AND MINDFULNESS PRACTICES TO TUNE INTO YOUR INNER VOICE

In our modern world, characterized by constant stimulation and relentless busyness, the whispers of our inner voice often get drowned out by the cacophony of external noise. To truly connect with our intuition, we must first learn to quiet the mind, creating a serene space where our inner wisdom can emerge. Meditation and mindfulness practices offer powerful tools for achieving this tranquility, enabling us to tune into the subtle signals of our intuition and navigate life's complexities with greater clarity and purpose.

Meditation, in its essence, is the practice of training the mind to focus and redirect thoughts. It involves creating a state of deep relaxation and inner stillness, allowing us to detach from the incessant chatter of our thoughts and emotions. Through regular meditation practice, we can cultivate a sense of inner peace, clarity, and heightened awareness, making us more receptive to the subtle whispers of our intuition.

Mindfulness, on the other hand, is the practice of paying non-judgmental attention to the present moment. It involves anchoring our awareness to the here and now, observing our thoughts, feelings, and bodily sensations without getting caught up in them. By cultivating mindfulness, we develop a greater sense of self-awareness, allowing us to recognize the subtle cues of our intuition and make choices that align with our true values and aspirations.

Together, meditation and mindfulness create a powerful synergy, working hand in hand to quiet the mind and awaken our intuitive faculties. By calming the turbulent waters of our thoughts and emotions, we create a fertile ground for our intuition to flourish.

The benefits of meditation and mindfulness practices are numerous and far-reaching. They have been shown to reduce stress, anxiety, and depression, improve sleep quality, boost creativity, and enhance overall well-being. Furthermore, they can strengthen our immune system, lower blood pressure, and even slow down the aging process.

However, the most profound benefit of meditation and mindfulness may lie in their ability to cultivate our intuition. By quieting the mind and creating a state of inner stillness, we allow our intuitive faculties to emerge from the depths of our subconscious. We become more attuned to our inner voice, more sensitive to the subtle signals and synchronicities that guide us on our path.

There are various forms of meditation and mindfulness practices, each with its unique approach and benefits. Some popular techniques include focused attention meditation, where we concentrate on a specific object or sensation, such as our breath or a mantra; open monitoring meditation, where we observe our thoughts and emotions without judgment; and loving-kindness meditation, where we cultivate feelings of compassion and goodwill towards ourselves and others.

Mindfulness can be integrated into our daily lives through simple practices such as mindful eating, walking, or listening. By bringing our full attention to the present moment, we can infuse our daily activities with a sense of awareness and intention, creating opportunities for intuitive insights to emerge.

The journey of quieting the mind and cultivating intuition is a lifelong endeavor. It requires patience, perseverance, and a willingness to explore the depths of our inner being. However, the rewards are immeasurable.

By making meditation and mindfulness a regular part of our lives, we can tap into a wellspring of wisdom and creativity, navigate life's challenges with greater ease, and live a more authentic, fulfilling, and purposeful life. We can discover the hidden treasures within ourselves, awaken our dormant intuition, and unleash our full potential.

As we embark on this journey, let us remember that the quiet mind is not an empty mind. It is a mind that is open, receptive, and attuned to the subtle whispers of our intuition. It is a mind that is connected to the deeper currents of life, the source of our creativity, wisdom, and joy.

ppp

Dreams are not just random firings of your neurons; they are messages from your subconscious mind, encoded in symbols and metaphors. Decipher their meaning, and you will unlock a treasure trove of intuitive wisdom.

SEVEN

Nature's Guidance: Spending Time in Nature to Connect with Your Intuition

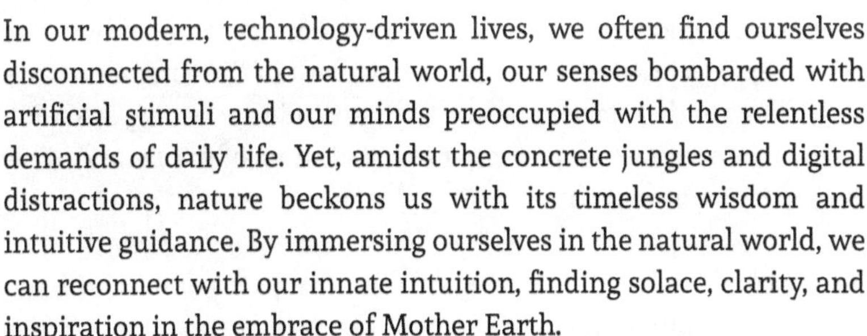

In our modern, technology-driven lives, we often find ourselves disconnected from the natural world, our senses bombarded with artificial stimuli and our minds preoccupied with the relentless demands of daily life. Yet, amidst the concrete jungles and digital distractions, nature beckons us with its timeless wisdom and intuitive guidance. By immersing ourselves in the natural world, we can reconnect with our innate intuition, finding solace, clarity, and inspiration in the embrace of Mother Earth.

Nature, in its infinite wisdom, holds a mirror to our souls, reflecting our deepest emotions, desires, and fears. The rustling leaves whisper secrets of resilience and adaptation, the flowing rivers teach us the art of surrender and letting go, and the majestic mountains inspire us to reach for our highest potential. By simply being in nature, we open ourselves up to a profound sense of interconnectedness, a realization that we are an integral part of a vast and intricate web of life.

Spending time in nature has a profound impact on our physical, mental, and emotional well-being. It has been scientifically proven to reduce stress, anxiety, and depression, boost creativity, and enhance our cognitive function. The Japanese practice of "Shinrin-yoku," or forest bathing, has gained worldwide recognition for its therapeutic benefits, promoting relaxation, mindfulness, and a deeper connection with nature.

However, the impact of nature on our intuition goes far beyond its physiological effects. By immersing ourselves in the natural world, we create space for our intuition to emerge from the depths of our subconscious. The quietude of a forest, the vastness of the ocean, or the gentle breeze on our skin can quiet the chatter of our minds, allowing us to tune into the subtle whispers of our inner wisdom.

Nature speaks to us in a language that transcends words, a language of sensations, emotions, and intuitive knowing. The scent of wildflowers may evoke a childhood memory, the sound of birdsong may inspire a creative idea, and the warmth of the sun on our face may fill us with a sense of peace and gratitude. By paying attention to these subtle cues, we can tap into the wisdom of nature and allow it to guide us on our path.

The natural world offers us a multitude of ways to connect with our intuition. A simple walk in the woods can be a profound meditative experience, allowing us to connect with the rhythm of our breath and the sensations of our body. Observing the intricate patterns of a spider web, the delicate dance of a butterfly, or the majestic flight of

an eagle can awaken a sense of awe and wonder, opening our hearts
and minds to the mysteries of the universe.

ᐁᐁᐁ

Your intuition journal is a sacred space, a sanctuary for your innermost thoughts and feelings. As you document your intuitive insights, you strengthen your connection to your inner wisdom and gain confidence in its guidance.

EIGHT

CREATIVE EXPRESSION: HOW ART, MUSIC, AND WRITING CAN UNLOCK YOUR INTUITION

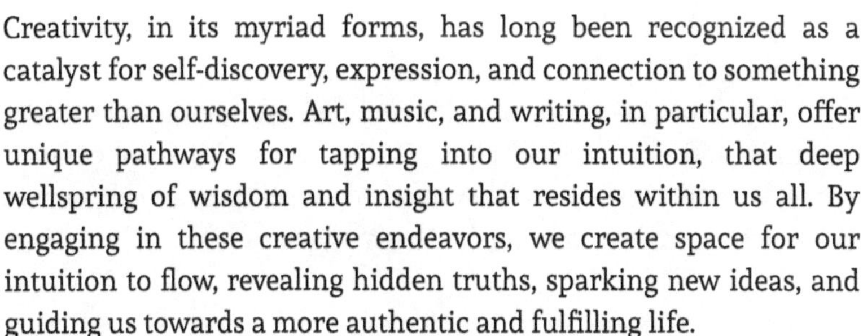

Creativity, in its myriad forms, has long been recognized as a catalyst for self-discovery, expression, and connection to something greater than ourselves. Art, music, and writing, in particular, offer unique pathways for tapping into our intuition, that deep wellspring of wisdom and insight that resides within us all. By engaging in these creative endeavors, we create space for our intuition to flow, revealing hidden truths, sparking new ideas, and guiding us towards a more authentic and fulfilling life.

At its core, creativity is the act of bringing something new into being, of transforming raw materials and ideas into tangible forms.

It is a process of exploration, experimentation, and self-expression, where we allow our imaginations to run wild and our hearts to speak their truth. When we engage in creative expression, we tap into our subconscious mind, accessing a wealth of emotions, memories, and experiences that may be hidden from our conscious awareness.

Art, in all its diverse forms, provides a powerful outlet for our intuition. Painting, sculpting, drawing, and other visual arts allow us to express ourselves non-verbally, bypassing the limitations of language and logic. As we engage with color, texture, and form, we enter a state of flow, where our intuition guides our hand and our heart leads the way.

Music, with its universal language of rhythm, melody, and harmony, has a profound impact on our emotions and subconscious mind. Listening to music can evoke a wide range of feelings, from joy and excitement to sadness and contemplation. Creating music, whether through playing an instrument, singing, or composing, allows us to channel our emotions and tap into our intuition. As we improvise, experiment, and explore new sounds, we open ourselves up to the wisdom of our inner voice.

Writing, the art of weaving words into meaningful narratives, can be a powerful tool for self-discovery and intuitive exploration. Journaling, poetry, fiction, and other forms of writing allow us to delve into our innermost thoughts and feelings, giving voice to our intuition and uncovering hidden truths. As we write, we create a space for our intuition to flow, revealing insights and perspectives that we may not have been consciously aware of.

The act of creating art, music, or writing can be a deeply meditative experience, quieting the mind and opening the heart. As we focus our attention on the creative process, we enter a state of flow, where time seems to dissolve and our intuition takes the lead. In this state, we are more receptive to the subtle whispers of our inner voice, the gentle nudges and insights that guide us on our path.

Moreover, the act of sharing our creative expressions with others can deepen our connection to our intuition. When we share our art, music, or writing with the world, we open ourselves up to feedback and validation, which can reinforce our intuitive sense of self and purpose. We also create opportunities for connection and collaboration, where we can learn from others and expand our creative horizons.

The link between creativity and intuition is not a one-way street. Just as creative expression can unlock our intuition, our intuition can also enhance our creativity. By trusting our gut feelings and following our creative impulses, we can tap into a wellspring of inspiration and generate new ideas that resonate with our audience.

In a world that often prioritizes logic and reason, creativity offers a counterbalance, a reminder that there are other ways of knowing and being. It invites us to explore the depths of our imagination, to embrace the unknown, and to trust the wisdom of our hearts.

So, if you're seeking to connect with your intuition, pick up a paintbrush, a musical instrument, or a pen. Allow yourself to be guided by your creative impulses, to experiment, to play, and to express yourself freely. In the act of creating, you may just discover a deeper connection to your inner voice, a wellspring of wisdom and insight that can guide you towards a more authentic and fulfilling life.

Whether you're a seasoned artist, a budding musician, or a novice writer, the act of creating can be a powerful tool for self-discovery and intuitive exploration. Embrace your creativity, trust your intuition, and allow your inner voice to guide you on your journey.

The possibilities are endless.

❧❧❧

When faced with a decision, consult your intuition. It will guide you towards choices that align with your values and lead to greater fulfillment. Trust your gut feeling, and you will find yourself on a path that resonates with your soul.

NINE

DREAM MESSAGES: INTERPRETING DREAMS AS A SOURCE OF INTUITIVE WISDOM

Dreams, those enigmatic nocturnal narratives that unfold in the theater of our minds, have captivated and perplexed humanity for millennia. Often dismissed as mere figments of our imagination or random firings of our neurons, dreams hold a deeper significance, serving as a conduit for our intuition, a portal to our subconscious wisdom. By learning to interpret the symbolism and messages embedded within our dreams, we can unlock a treasure trove of insights, guidance, and self-awareness.

Throughout history, dreams have been revered as a source of divine revelation, prophetic visions, and intuitive guidance. Ancient civilizations, from the Egyptians to the Greeks, believed that dreams were messages from the gods, offering glimpses into the future and revealing hidden truths about the human condition. Shamans and spiritual leaders sought guidance from their dreams, using them to diagnose illnesses, resolve conflicts, and make important decisions.

While modern science may offer a more rational explanation for the phenomenon of dreaming, it does not negate its potential for intuitive insight. In fact, research has shown that dreams play a crucial role in memory consolidation, emotional processing, and problem-solving. They provide a safe space for our subconscious minds to explore complex issues, work through unresolved conflicts, and offer creative solutions to challenges we face in our waking lives.

The language of dreams is often symbolic and metaphorical, requiring us to delve beyond the literal meaning of the images and events that unfold in our nocturnal narratives. A snake, for example, may represent transformation and renewal, while a flying dream may symbolize a desire for freedom and transcendence.

Interpreting dreams is a deeply personal and intuitive process. There is no one-size-fits-all approach, as the meaning of a dream can vary depending on the individual's personal experiences, cultural background, and emotional state. However, there are several key principles and techniques that can help us decipher the messages hidden within our dreams.

One approach is to pay attention to the emotions evoked by the dream. How did the dream make you feel? Were you happy, sad, scared, or excited? These emotions can offer valuable clues about the underlying meaning of the dream.

Another approach is to identify recurring themes or symbols in your dreams. Do you frequently dream about flying, falling, being chased, or encountering certain animals or objects? These recurring motifs may represent unresolved issues or recurring patterns in your life that need to be addressed.

Keeping a dream journal can be a powerful tool for dream interpretation. By recording your dreams as soon as you wake up, you can capture the details and emotions of the dream while they are still fresh in your mind. Reviewing your dream journal over time can reveal patterns and insights that you might not have noticed otherwise.

Seeking guidance from a professional dream interpreter can also be helpful. These experts can offer a fresh perspective and provide insights into the symbolism and archetypes that appear in your dreams.

It is important to note that not all dreams are prophetic or predictive. Some dreams may simply be a reflection of our daily experiences, anxieties, or desires. However, even these seemingly mundane dreams can offer valuable insights into our subconscious minds and help us understand our deepest fears and motivations.

By embracing our dreams as a source of intuitive wisdom, we open ourselves up to a deeper understanding of ourselves and the world around us. We can learn to trust our intuition, follow our inner guidance, and make choices that align with our true values and aspirations.

The journey of dream interpretation is a lifelong adventure, filled with surprises, insights, and self-discovery. As we learn to decode the language of our dreams, we unlock a hidden dimension of our consciousness, a realm of infinite possibilities and profound wisdom.

So, the next time you awaken from a dream, take a moment to reflect on its meaning. Write down your dream, explore the emotions it evoked, and consider the symbolism it contains. Allow your intuition to guide you, and trust that your dreams hold a message for you, a message that can illuminate your path and lead you towards a more fulfilling life.

❧❧❧

In relationships, intuition can be your most valuable ally. It helps you discern authenticity, navigate conflicts, and deepen your connection with loved ones. Trust its whispers, and you will build relationships that nourish your spirit.

TEN

INTUITION JOURNAL: DOCUMENTING YOUR INTUITIVE INSIGHTS TO STRENGTHEN YOUR CONNECTION

An intuition journal, a simple yet powerful tool, can be your personal guidebook on the journey of self-discovery and intuitive awakening. It serves as a sacred space to document your intuitive insights, track their evolution, and deepen your connection to your inner wisdom. By consistently recording your hunches, gut feelings, and flashes of insight, you not only validate your intuition but also strengthen its presence in your life.

At its core, an intuition journal is a personal record of your intuitive experiences. It can be a physical notebook, a digital document, or even a voice recording app. The key is to choose a format that feels comfortable and accessible to you, one that encourages you to express yourself freely and honestly.

There is no right or wrong way to keep an intuition journal. Some people prefer to write detailed accounts of their intuitive experiences, including the circumstances, emotions, and insights involved. Others may simply jot down keywords, phrases, or symbols that represent their intuitive nudges. The most important thing is to be consistent and to write from the heart.

The act of writing itself can be a powerful tool for accessing and strengthening our intuition. As we put pen to paper or fingers to keyboard, we engage our subconscious mind, allowing intuitive insights to surface from the depths of our awareness. The physical act of writing can also help us to clarify our thoughts and feelings, making it easier to discern the subtle whispers of our intuition.

By documenting our intuitive experiences in a journal, we create a valuable resource for self-reflection and growth. We can look back on our entries and identify patterns, themes, and recurring symbols. We can also track the accuracy of our intuitive insights, gaining confidence in our ability to discern truth from falsehood.

The intuition journal can also serve as a source of inspiration and guidance. When we feel lost or uncertain, we can turn to our journal for reminders of past intuitive insights that have proven to be accurate and helpful. We can also use our journal to track our progress on our intuitive journey, celebrating our successes and learning from our mistakes.

In addition to documenting our intuitive experiences, we can also use our intuition journal to set intentions, ask questions, and explore our deepest desires and fears. By engaging with our journal in a conscious and intentional way, we can create a powerful dialogue with our intuition, deepening our connection to this inner source of wisdom.

The intuition journal is not just a passive record of our intuitive experiences; it is an active tool for cultivating and strengthening our intuition. By regularly engaging with our journal, we create a positive feedback loop that reinforces our intuitive abilities and helps us to trust our inner voice.

As we document our intuitive insights, we begin to notice the subtle ways in which our intuition manifests in our lives. We become more attuned to the synchronicities, coincidences, and signs that are constantly guiding us on our path. We also develop a greater sense of trust in our own judgment, knowing that we have a reliable source of inner wisdom to guide us.

The intuition journal is a personal journey of self-discovery and intuitive exploration. It is a sacred space where we can connect with our innermost selves, tap into our intuition, and unleash our full potential. By embracing the power of the intuition journal, we can cultivate a deeper connection to our inner wisdom and live a more authentic, fulfilling, and purposeful life.

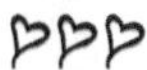

Your career is not just a means to an end; it is an expression of your soul's purpose. Let your intuition guide you towards work that ignites your passion and fulfills your deepest desires.

ELEVEN

Decision Making: Using your intuition to make choices that align with your values

Decision-making, a fundamental aspect of human existence, is often fraught with uncertainty, doubt, and conflicting emotions. While logic and reason play a crucial role in analyzing options and weighing consequences, there is another powerful force at play, one that operates beneath the surface of our conscious awareness: intuition. This inner voice, this gut feeling, can guide us towards choices that align with our deepest values, leading to a more authentic and fulfilling life.

Intuition, often described as a "knowing without knowing why," is a form of non-rational cognition that arises from the depths of our subconscious mind. It is a synthesis of our past experiences, emotions, beliefs, and values, distilled into a subtle yet powerful sense of what feels right or wrong. Unlike logical reasoning, which relies on conscious analysis and deliberation, intuition operates more spontaneously and effortlessly, offering us guidance in the blink of an eye.

When faced with a decision, our intuition can manifest in various ways. It might be a subtle feeling of unease or excitement, a gut-wrenching sensation, or a sudden flash of insight. It might also appear as a hunch, a nagging thought, or a recurring dream. The key is to recognize these intuitive signals and trust them as valuable sources of information.

Our intuition is not infallible, of course. It can be influenced by our biases, fears, and past traumas. However, when cultivated and honed, it can become a reliable compass, guiding us towards choices that are in alignment with our deepest values and aspirations.

Using our intuition in decision-making involves a delicate dance between our head and our heart. We must learn to balance the logical analysis of facts and figures with the intuitive wisdom that resides within us. This requires us to quiet our minds, listen to our bodies, and trust our gut feelings.

One way to access our intuition is to simply ask ourselves, "What feels right?" This simple question can often cut through the clutter of conflicting thoughts and emotions and reveal a clear path forward. We can also try visualizing ourselves in different scenarios and paying attention to how each option makes us feel. If a particular choice elicits a sense of joy, excitement, or peace, it is likely aligned with our values.

Another way to tap into our intuition is to pay attention to our body's signals. Our bodies are constantly communicating with us, sending subtle cues and messages that can guide our decision-making. A tightness in the chest may indicate that a particular choice is not in alignment with our values, while a sense of lightness and ease may suggest that we are on the right track.

Meditation and mindfulness practices can also help us to cultivate our intuition. By quieting our minds and creating space for inner stillness, we allow our intuition to emerge from the depths of our subconscious. Regular meditation practice can also help us to develop a greater sense of self-awareness, making it easier to recognize and interpret our intuitive signals.

It is important to note that intuition is not a substitute for logical reasoning. In many situations, it is essential to gather information, analyze data, and weigh the pros and cons of different options. However, intuition can complement and enhance our logical decision-making process. By incorporating both intuitive and rational approaches, we can make more informed, holistic, and ultimately, more satisfying choices.

Ultimately, using our intuition to make choices that align with our values is a journey of self-discovery and self-trust. It involves learning to listen to our inner voice, to decipher the subtle messages of our bodies, and to trust our gut feelings. By embracing our intuition as a valuable guide, we can navigate life's challenges with greater clarity, confidence, and authenticity.

Self-care is not a luxury but a necessity. Your intuition knows what your body, mind, and spirit need to thrive. Listen to its whispers and honor your needs for rest, nourishment, and joy.

TWELVE

RELATIONSHIPS: INTUITIVE INSIGHTS FOR BUILDING HEALTHY AND FULFILLING CONNECTIONS

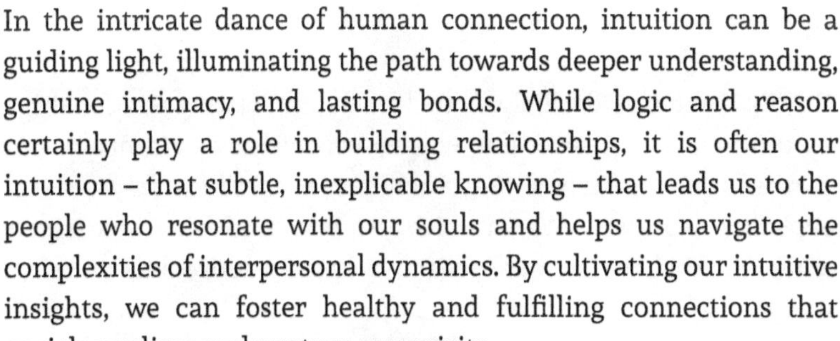

In the intricate dance of human connection, intuition can be a guiding light, illuminating the path towards deeper understanding, genuine intimacy, and lasting bonds. While logic and reason certainly play a role in building relationships, it is often our intuition – that subtle, inexplicable knowing – that leads us to the people who resonate with our souls and helps us navigate the complexities of interpersonal dynamics. By cultivating our intuitive insights, we can foster healthy and fulfilling connections that enrich our lives and nurture our spirits.

Intuition in relationships can manifest in various ways. It might be a gut feeling about someone's character, a sense of ease or discomfort in their presence, or a sudden flash of insight into their motivations and desires. It might also be a knowingness that transcends words, a deep sense of connection that defies explanation. These intuitive insights, often dismissed as mere whims or fancies, can offer valuable guidance in navigating the complexities of interpersonal relationships.

One of the most powerful ways in which intuition can guide us in relationships is by helping us choose the right people to connect with. Our intuition can often sense whether someone is trustworthy, supportive, and aligned with our values, even before we have gathered any concrete evidence. That initial spark of attraction, the feeling of being seen and understood, or the sense of ease and comfort in someone's presence – these are all signs that our intuition is pointing us towards a potentially meaningful connection.

Intuition can also help us navigate the inevitable challenges that arise in any relationship. When conflicts arise, our intuition can guide us towards compassionate communication, helping us to express our needs and concerns in a way that fosters understanding and resolution. It can also help us to discern when it is time to let go of a relationship that no longer serves us, allowing us to move on with grace and dignity.

Our intuition can also help us to deepen our existing relationships. By tuning into our intuition, we can become more attuned to our partner's needs, desires, and emotions, even when they are not explicitly expressed. We can also use our intuition to anticipate potential conflicts and take proactive steps to address them before they escalate.

Cultivating our intuition in relationships requires us to quiet our minds, listen to our bodies, and trust our gut feelings. Meditation, mindfulness, and other contemplative practices can help us to develop this inner awareness and sensitivity. We can also practice active listening, paying attention to both verbal and nonverbal cues, and allowing our intuition to guide our responses.

It is important to note that intuition is not a substitute for healthy communication and boundaries. We must still be willing to express our needs, set limits, and hold others accountable for their actions. However, by integrating intuition into our relational toolbox, we can navigate the complexities of human connection with greater ease, grace, and authenticity.

Intuition can also help us to cultivate a deeper sense of intimacy and connection in our relationships. By trusting our intuition, we can become more vulnerable and open with our partners, sharing our deepest fears, desires, and dreams. We can also use our intuition to sense when our partners need our support, offering them love, compassion, and understanding.

Ultimately, using intuition in relationships is about learning to trust ourselves and our inner wisdom. It is about recognizing that we have a deep well of knowledge and insight within us, and that this knowledge can guide us towards healthier, happier, and more fulfilling connections.

By embracing our intuition as a valuable tool in relationships, we can create a life filled with love, joy, and meaning. We can cultivate deeper connections with our partners, family, friends, and colleagues, and we can build a community that supports us on our journey of personal growth and transformation.

In the tapestry of human connection, intuition is the golden thread that weaves together our hearts, minds, and souls. It is the compass that guides us towards authentic relationships, the key that unlocks the door to deeper intimacy, and the light that illuminates the path towards a more loving and connected world.

ᗒᗒᗒ

In times of crisis, your intuition can be your anchor, guiding you through the storm with clarity and resilience. Trust its wisdom, and you will emerge stronger, wiser, and more connected to your true self.

THIRTEEN

Career Path: Finding work that resonates with your inner purpose

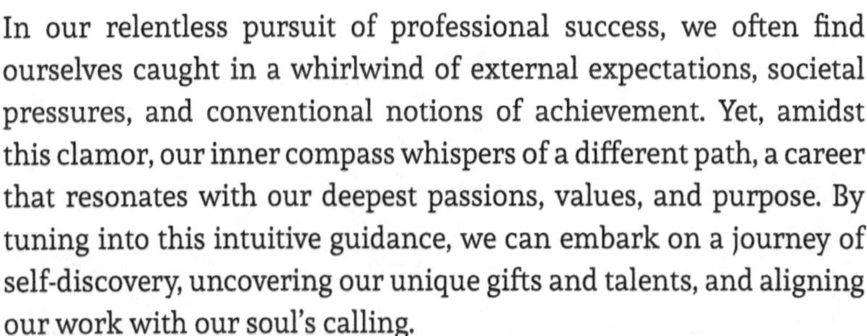

In our relentless pursuit of professional success, we often find ourselves caught in a whirlwind of external expectations, societal pressures, and conventional notions of achievement. Yet, amidst this clamor, our inner compass whispers of a different path, a career that resonates with our deepest passions, values, and purpose. By tuning into this intuitive guidance, we can embark on a journey of self-discovery, uncovering our unique gifts and talents, and aligning our work with our soul's calling.

The quest for a fulfilling career is more than just finding a job that pays the bills or offers social status. It is about finding work that ignites our passions, challenges our intellect, and allows us to make a meaningful contribution to the world. It is about discovering our unique purpose and aligning our professional endeavors with our core values.

Our intuition, that inner voice that speaks to us through subtle feelings, hunches, and insights, can be a powerful guide on this journey. It can help us to identify our true passions, recognize our unique gifts, and navigate the often-confusing landscape of career choices.

One way in which intuition can guide us on our career path is by helping us to identify our passions. What activities make us feel alive, energized, and fulfilled? What are we naturally drawn to, even when there is no external reward or recognition? By paying attention to these intuitive pulls, we can gain valuable insights into our innate talents and interests.

Our intuition can also help us to recognize our unique gifts and strengths. What are we naturally good at? What do others come to us for help with? What do we enjoy doing so much that we lose track of time? By identifying our strengths and weaknesses, we can choose a career path that leverages our talents and allows us to shine.

Intuition can also guide us in navigating the often-confusing landscape of career choices. When faced with multiple options, our intuition can help us to discern which path is most aligned with our values and aspirations. It can also help us to identify potential pitfalls or challenges that we may encounter along the way.

The process of finding work that resonates with our inner purpose is not always easy. It requires us to quiet our minds, listen to our hearts, and trust our intuition. It may also involve taking risks, stepping outside of our comfort zones, and challenging societal expectations. However, the rewards of pursuing a career that is aligned with our soul's calling are immeasurable.

When we do work that we love, we are more likely to be engaged, motivated, and productive. We are also more likely to experience a sense of purpose and meaning in our lives. This, in turn, can lead to greater happiness, well-being, and overall life satisfaction.

There are various practices that can help us to connect with our intuition and discover our career path. Meditation, mindfulness, and other forms of contemplative practice can help us to quiet our minds and access our inner wisdom. Journaling, vision boards, and other creative expressions can also help us to clarify our goals and aspirations.

Seeking guidance from mentors, coaches, and career counselors can also be helpful. These professionals can offer valuable insights and support as we navigate our career journey. They can also help us to identify our blind spots and overcome any obstacles that we may encounter along the way.

Ultimately, finding work that resonates with our inner purpose is a journey of self-discovery and self-expression. It is about connecting with our passions, recognizing our unique gifts, and aligning our professional endeavors with our core values. By trusting our intuition and following our hearts, we can create a career that is not only financially rewarding but also personally fulfilling and meaningful.

ᛈᛈᛈ

Don't let fear or doubt cloud your intuitive vision. Embrace your intuition as a trusted friend, a guide who wants nothing more than for you to flourish.

FOURTEEN

SELF-CARE: HONORING YOUR INTUITIVE NEEDS FOR REST, NOURISHMENT, AND JOY

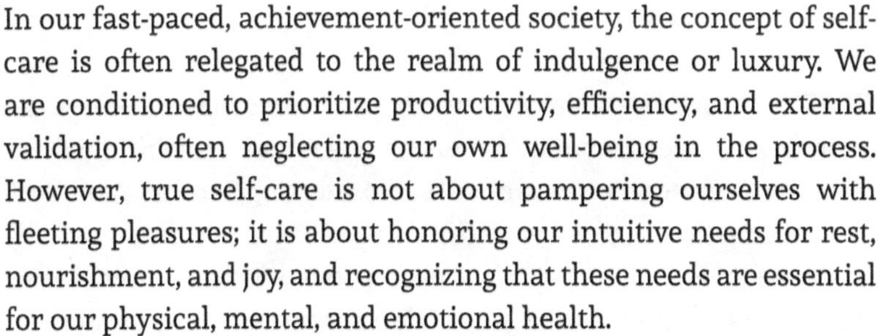

In our fast-paced, achievement-oriented society, the concept of self-care is often relegated to the realm of indulgence or luxury. We are conditioned to prioritize productivity, efficiency, and external validation, often neglecting our own well-being in the process. However, true self-care is not about pampering ourselves with fleeting pleasures; it is about honoring our intuitive needs for rest, nourishment, and joy, and recognizing that these needs are essential for our physical, mental, and emotional health.

Our bodies are intricately designed, with an innate wisdom that guides us towards what we need to thrive. This wisdom manifests in the form of subtle cues and signals, such as fatigue, hunger, and a yearning for connection or creativity. When we ignore these signals, we not only deplete our energy reserves but also disconnect from our intuition, the inner voice that guides us towards a more fulfilling life.

Rest, a fundamental human need, is often undervalued in our culture. We are bombarded with messages that equate busyness with success and productivity with worth. However, rest is not a sign of weakness or laziness; it is an essential component of our well-being. When we rest, we allow our bodies and minds to recharge, repair, and rejuvenate. We create space for creativity, insight, and inspiration to emerge.

Our intuition often speaks to us through our need for rest. When we feel tired, drained, or overwhelmed, it is a sign that we need to slow down, take a break, and replenish our energy reserves. This might mean getting a good night's sleep, taking a nap, or simply allowing ourselves to relax and do nothing.

Nourishment, another essential component of self-care, extends beyond the physical realm. While it is important to nourish our bodies with healthy food and water, we must also nourish our minds and spirits with positive thoughts, inspiring ideas, and meaningful connections.

Our intuition can guide us towards the type of nourishment we need in any given moment. When we feel emotionally drained, we might seek solace in a warm bath, a comforting conversation with a loved one, or a quiet walk in nature. When we feel mentally exhausted, we might turn to a good book, a stimulating documentary, or a creative project that sparks our imagination.

Joy, often elusive in our busy lives, is a fundamental human need. It is the feeling of delight, pleasure, and satisfaction that arises when we engage in activities that we love, connect with people we care about, or simply appreciate the beauty of the world around us.

Our intuition can be a powerful guide towards joy. When we feel stuck, bored, or uninspired, it is a sign that we need to inject more joy into our lives. This might mean pursuing a hobby, spending time with loved ones, or simply doing something that makes us laugh.

By honoring our intuitive needs for rest, nourishment, and joy, we not only improve our physical, mental, and emotional health, but we also deepen our connection to our intuition. When we are well-rested, nourished, and joyful, we are more receptive to the subtle whispers of our inner voice, the gentle nudges that guide us towards our highest good.

Practicing intuitive self-care requires us to slow down, listen to our bodies, and trust our gut feelings. It involves paying attention to the subtle signals that our bodies are sending us and responding to them with compassion and kindness. It also means setting boundaries, saying no to things that drain us, and prioritizing activities that bring us joy and fulfillment.

Intuitive self-care is not a one-size-fits-all approach. What works for one person may not work for another. The key is to experiment, to try different things, and to discover what nourishes and replenishes you on a deep level.

As you embark on your journey of intuitive self-care, remember that it is an ongoing process. Your needs will change and evolve over time, and it is important to be flexible and adaptable in your approach.

By making self-care a priority, you not only improve your own well-being, but you also create a ripple effect that positively impacts those around you. When you are well-rested, nourished, and joyful, you are more likely to be patient, compassionate, and supportive of others. You are also more likely to inspire others to prioritize their own self-care, creating a more loving and supportive world for all.

ϸϸϸ

Your intuition is not a static entity; it evolves and matures alongside you. As you learn and grow, so too does your intuition. Embrace its evolution and trust its ever-expanding wisdom.

FIFTEEN

Intuition in Crisis: How your inner compass can guide you through challenging times

In the tempestuous storms of life, when the winds of change howl and the waves of adversity crash around us, our intuition emerges as a steadfast compass, guiding us through the turbulent seas towards calmer waters. During times of crisis, when logic and reason may falter, our intuition, that deep-seated wisdom within, can offer solace, clarity, and direction, helping us navigate the challenges with resilience and grace.

Crises, whether personal or global, can shake us to our core, leaving us feeling disoriented, overwhelmed, and uncertain. The familiar ground beneath our feet may crumble, and the future may seem shrouded in darkness. It is precisely in these moments of uncertainty that our intuition can shine its brightest, illuminating a path forward when all other lights seem to have dimmed.

Our intuition, often described as a gut feeling or a hunch, is a form of non-rational cognition that arises from the depths of our subconscious mind. It is a synthesis of our past experiences, emotions, beliefs, and values, distilled into a subtle yet powerful sense of what feels right or wrong. In times of crisis, when our rational mind may be overwhelmed by fear and anxiety, our intuition can offer a clear and decisive voice, guiding us towards the best course of action.

One way in which intuition can guide us through crisis is by helping us to prioritize our needs and values. In the midst of chaos and uncertainty, it can be easy to lose sight of what truly matters. Our intuition can help us to reconnect with our core values, reminding us of what is truly important and guiding us towards choices that align with our authentic selves.

Intuition can also help us to identify potential dangers and opportunities. In times of crisis, our senses are heightened, and our intuition may pick up on subtle cues and signals that our conscious mind may miss. This heightened awareness can help us to anticipate potential threats and take proactive steps to protect ourselves. It can also help us to identify hidden opportunities for growth and transformation that may arise from the ashes of adversity.

Another way in which intuition can guide us through crisis is by offering us comfort and solace. In the face of loss, grief, or trauma, our intuition can connect us to a deeper sense of meaning and purpose. It can remind us of our resilience, our strength, and our capacity for healing. It can also offer us glimpses of hope and possibility, even in the darkest of times.

Cultivating our intuition in times of crisis requires us to quiet our minds, listen to our bodies, and trust our gut feelings. Meditation, mindfulness, and other contemplative practices can help us to create space for our intuition to emerge. It is also important to surround ourselves with supportive people who can offer us encouragement and guidance.

When faced with a crisis, it is important to remember that we are not alone. We are part of a vast interconnected web of life, and we can draw upon the strength and wisdom of this interconnectedness to navigate through challenging times. Our intuition can help us to tap into this collective wisdom, guiding us towards the resources and support we need to heal and thrive.

The journey through crisis is not always easy. It may involve pain, loss, and grief. However, by trusting our intuition and allowing it to guide us, we can emerge from the storm stronger, wiser, and more resilient. We can discover new depths of compassion, courage, and resilience within ourselves, and we can forge a path towards a brighter future.

In the tapestry of life, crises are the threads that weave together the fabric of our experiences. They challenge us, stretch us, and ultimately, transform us. By embracing our intuition as a trusted guide, we can navigate these challenges with grace, courage, and wisdom, emerging from the crucible of crisis as more authentic, resilient, and compassionate human beings.

❧❧❧

Connecting with others who value intuitive guidance can amplify your own intuition. Share your experiences, learn from others, and together, create a community that celebrates the power of intuition.

SIXTEEN

INTUITION MYTHS: DISPELLING COMMON MISCONCEPTIONS ABOUT INTUITION

Intuition, that elusive whisper of inner knowing, has been a source of fascination and misunderstanding for centuries. Often shrouded in mystique and misconceptions, it is time to shed light on the truth about intuition, dispelling the common myths that have obscured its true nature and hindered its acceptance as a valuable tool for navigating life's complexities.

One of the most prevalent myths surrounding intuition is that it is a rare gift bestowed upon a select few, a mystical power reserved for psychics, mediums, or spiritual gurus. This notion couldn't be further from the truth. Intuition is a universal human faculty, an innate capacity that resides within each and every one of us. While some individuals may have naturally stronger intuitive abilities, everyone has the potential to develop and cultivate their intuition through practice and self-awareness.

Another common misconception is that intuition is synonymous with psychic abilities or premonitions. While intuition can sometimes offer glimpses into the future or provide insights into situations beyond our immediate awareness, it is not solely limited to these phenomena. Intuition encompasses a wide range of experiences, from subtle hunches and gut feelings to profound moments of clarity and insight. It is a multi-faceted tool that can be applied to various aspects of our lives, from decision-making and problem-solving to relationships and creativity.

Furthermore, intuition is often mistaken for mere guesswork or wishful thinking. While intuitive insights may sometimes appear as fleeting thoughts or spontaneous ideas, they are not simply random guesses. Intuition draws upon a vast reservoir of subconscious knowledge and experience, synthesizing information from multiple sources to provide us with a holistic understanding of a situation. It is a form of intelligence that goes beyond logic and reason, tapping into a deeper level of awareness and understanding.

Another common myth is that intuition is always right. While intuition can offer valuable guidance, it is not infallible. Like any other skill, it requires practice and discernment to refine and hone its accuracy. Sometimes, our intuition may be clouded by our own biases, fears, or desires. It is important to approach intuitive insights with a healthy dose of skepticism and to test their validity through further exploration and reflection.

The myth that intuition is antithetical to logic and reason is also widespread. In reality, intuition and logic are complementary forces, each offering unique perspectives and insights. While logic relies on analysis, deduction, and evidence, intuition taps into a deeper level of knowing that transcends the rational mind. By integrating both intuition and logic, we can make more informed, holistic, and ultimately, more effective decisions.

Another misconception about intuition is that it is a passive process, something that simply happens to us without our conscious involvement. In reality, intuition is a skill that can be cultivated and strengthened through practice and self-awareness. By paying attention to our inner voice, practicing mindfulness, and engaging in activities that stimulate our creativity, we can enhance our intuitive abilities and harness their power to navigate life's challenges and opportunities.

The myth that intuition is solely a feminine trait is also a prevalent misconception. While some studies have suggested that women may be more in touch with their intuition than men, this is not a hard and fast rule. Intuition is a universal human faculty, and both men and women can develop and utilize their intuitive abilities.

Finally, it is important to dispel the myth that intuition is a purely spiritual or mystical phenomenon. While intuition can certainly play a role in our spiritual lives, it is not confined to the realm of religion or spirituality. Intuition is a natural human capacity that can be harnessed by anyone, regardless of their beliefs or worldview.

By dispelling these common myths about intuition, we can reclaim its rightful place as a valuable tool for personal growth, decision-making, and navigating life's complexities. Whether we are seeking guidance on a career path, a relationship, or a personal challenge, our intuition can offer valuable insights and support. By learning to trust our inner voice and cultivate our intuitive abilities, we can unlock a deeper level of wisdom and understanding, leading to a more fulfilling and purposeful life.

ᐅᐅᐅ

Intuition is not antithetical to logic and reason; it is a complementary force that can enhance your decision-making and problem-solving skills. Integrate both, and you will unlock a deeper understanding of yourself and the world.

SEVENTEEN

INTUITION BLOCKS: IDENTIFYING AND OVERCOMING OBSTACLES TO YOUR INTUITION

Intuition, that gentle whisper of inner wisdom, can be a powerful guide in navigating life's complexities. However, various obstacles, both internal and external, can cloud our intuitive vision, hindering our ability to access and trust this valuable source of guidance. By identifying and overcoming these intuition blocks, we can reclaim our innate capacity for insight and make more aligned choices in life.

One of the most common intuition blocks is overthinking, the relentless chatter of our minds that drowns out the subtle whispers of our inner voice. When we constantly analyze, rationalize, and second-guess ourselves, we create a mental barrier that prevents our intuition from surfacing. To overcome this block, we can practice mindfulness techniques that help us to quiet the mind, such as meditation, yoga, or spending time in nature. By cultivating a state of inner stillness, we create space for our intuition to emerge and guide us.

Another significant obstacle to intuition is fear. Fear of the unknown, fear of making mistakes, fear of judgment from others – these can all paralyze our intuitive faculties and prevent us from taking risks or following our gut feelings. To overcome fear, we need to cultivate courage and self-trust. We can do this by facing our fears head-on, practicing self-compassion, and reminding ourselves that mistakes are opportunities for growth and learning.

Negative self-talk, the inner critic that constantly undermines our confidence and self-worth, can also block our intuition. When we doubt ourselves and our abilities, we create a self-fulfilling prophecy that reinforces our insecurities and limits our potential. To overcome negative self-talk, we can practice positive affirmations, challenge our limiting beliefs, and surround ourselves with supportive people who believe in us.

Stress and overwhelm are other common culprits that can hinder our intuition. When we are constantly bombarded with stimuli and demands, our nervous system goes into fight-or-flight mode, making it difficult to access our intuition. To overcome stress and overwhelm, we need to prioritize self-care and create space for rest and relaxation. This might involve taking breaks throughout the day, practicing relaxation techniques like deep breathing or progressive muscle relaxation, or engaging in activities that bring us joy and peace.

External influences, such as societal expectations, cultural norms, and the opinions of others, can also create barriers to our intuition. We may feel pressured to conform to certain standards or to follow a path that is not aligned with our true selves. To overcome these external influences, we need to develop a strong sense of self and a willingness to challenge the status quo. We can also seek out supportive communities and mentors who can encourage us to follow our own path and trust our intuition.

Physical factors, such as fatigue, illness, or hormonal imbalances, can also affect our intuitive abilities. When our bodies are not functioning optimally, it can be difficult to access our intuition. To overcome these physical barriers, we need to prioritize our health and well-being. This might involve eating a healthy diet, getting regular exercise, and ensuring that we get enough sleep.

In addition to these specific blocks, there are other subtle factors that can hinder our intuition, such as a lack of self-awareness, a disconnection from our bodies, and a lack of trust in our own inner wisdom. By cultivating self-awareness, practicing embodiment techniques, and developing a deeper connection to our intuition, we can gradually overcome these obstacles and unlock our full intuitive potential.

The journey of identifying and overcoming intuition blocks is a personal one, unique to each individual. It requires self-reflection, honesty, and a willingness to confront our fears and limitations. However, the rewards of this journey are immeasurable. By clearing away the obstacles to our intuition, we can access a wellspring of wisdom and guidance that can lead us to a more authentic, fulfilling, and purposeful life.

❧❧❧

Your intuition is your unique gift, a reflection of your individual journey and experiences. Embrace its nuances, trust its guidance, and allow it to illuminate your path.

EIGHTEEN

INTUITION COMMUNITY: CONNECTING WITH OTHERS WHO VALUE INTUITIVE GUIDANCE

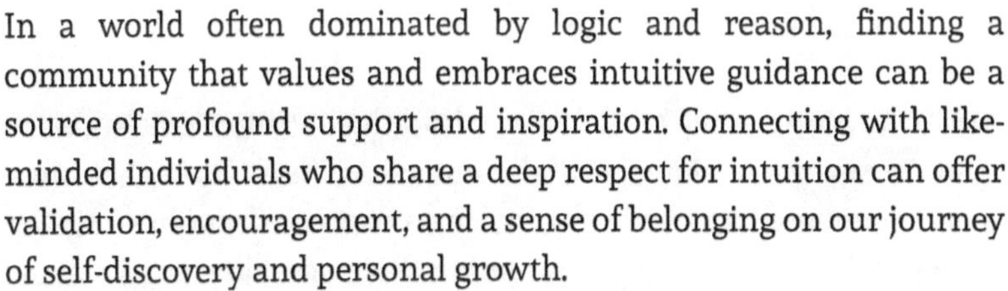

In a world often dominated by logic and reason, finding a community that values and embraces intuitive guidance can be a source of profound support and inspiration. Connecting with like-minded individuals who share a deep respect for intuition can offer validation, encouragement, and a sense of belonging on our journey of self-discovery and personal growth.

Such a community can take many forms. It could be a local group that meets regularly for meditation, discussion, and shared experiences. It might be an online forum or social media group where members can connect, share insights, and offer support to one another. Or it could be a network of friends, family members, or colleagues who share a common interest in intuition and its many applications.

The benefits of connecting with an intuition community are numerous and far-reaching. Firstly, it provides a safe and supportive space for individuals to explore and develop their intuitive abilities. In a world that often dismisses or belittles intuition, having a community that validates and encourages our intuitive explorations can be immensely empowering.

Furthermore, connecting with others who value intuitive guidance can deepen our understanding of intuition itself. By sharing our experiences, insights, and challenges with others, we can gain new perspectives, learn new techniques, and expand our knowledge of this fascinating field. We can also receive feedback and support from others, helping us to refine our intuitive skills and navigate the inevitable ups and downs of our intuitive journey.

An intuition community can also serve as a source of inspiration and motivation. When we see others embracing their intuition and using it to create positive change in their lives, it can ignite a spark of inspiration within us. We may be inspired to try new things, take risks, or step outside of our comfort zones, knowing that we have a supportive community to cheer us on.

Moreover, connecting with others who value intuitive guidance can foster a sense of belonging and connection. In a world that often feels fragmented and isolating, finding a community of like-minded individuals can be deeply nourishing. We can share our joys and sorrows, our triumphs and setbacks, knowing that we are not alone on our journey.

Building an intuition community can be as simple as inviting a few friends over for a shared meditation or intuitive practice. It could also involve joining an existing group or creating a new one online or in person. The key is to find a group that resonates with your values and interests, and that offers a safe and supportive space for exploration and growth.

Once you have found your community, it is important to actively participate and contribute to its growth. This might involve sharing your own experiences, offering support to others, or organizing events and activities. By actively engaging with your community, you not only benefit from the collective wisdom and support, but you also contribute to the creation of a vibrant and thriving space for intuitive exploration.

Connecting with others who value intuitive guidance is not only beneficial for our personal growth, but it also has the potential to create positive change in the world. When we come together as a community, we can amplify our intuitive voices, advocate for a more intuitive approach to life, and inspire others to embrace their own inner wisdom.

Whether you are a seasoned intuitive or just beginning to explore this fascinating realm, connecting with a community that values intuitive guidance can be a transformative experience. It can offer you the support, encouragement, and inspiration you need to deepen your connection to your intuition and live a more authentic, fulfilling, and purposeful life.

Don't be afraid to make mistakes on your intuitive journey. Each misstep is a learning opportunity, a chance to refine your skills and deepen your connection to your inner wisdom.

NINETEEN

THE INTUITIVE EVOLUTION: HOW YOUR INTUITION DEVELOPS OVER TIME

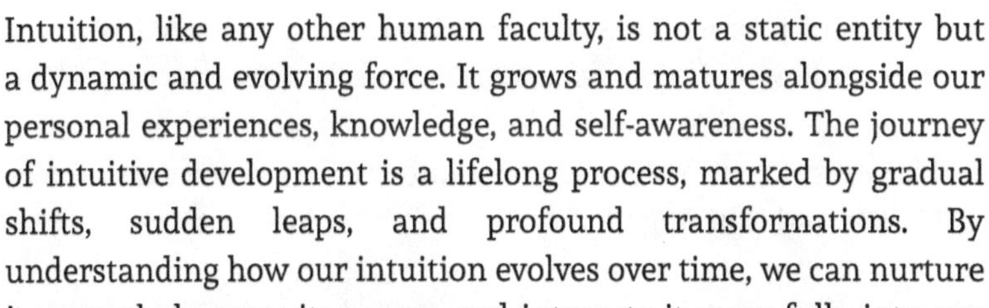

Intuition, like any other human faculty, is not a static entity but a dynamic and evolving force. It grows and matures alongside our personal experiences, knowledge, and self-awareness. The journey of intuitive development is a lifelong process, marked by gradual shifts, sudden leaps, and profound transformations. By understanding how our intuition evolves over time, we can nurture its growth, harness its power, and integrate it more fully into our lives.

In the early stages of life, our intuition manifests primarily as instinctual impulses and gut feelings. Young children often exhibit a remarkable ability to sense danger, discomfort, or authenticity in others, even without conscious reasoning or analysis. This innate sense of knowing is a survival mechanism, honed through millennia of evolution to protect us from harm and guide us towards safety and well-being.

As we grow and mature, our intuition begins to intertwine with our cognitive and emotional development. We learn to differentiate between our intuitive impulses and our conditioned responses, discerning the genuine whispers of our inner wisdom from the echoes of societal expectations and limiting beliefs. This process of discernment requires self-awareness, introspection, and a willingness to challenge our assumptions and preconceived notions.

With time and experience, our intuition becomes more refined and nuanced. We begin to recognize the subtle signs and synchronicities that guide us on our path, the seemingly random events that lead us to unexpected opportunities and meaningful connections. We also develop a greater capacity for empathy and compassion, allowing us to intuit the needs and emotions of others with greater accuracy and sensitivity.

As we continue to cultivate our intuition, we may experience moments of profound insight and clarity, where the veil between our conscious and subconscious minds seems to lift. These moments of intuitive awakening can be transformative, revealing hidden truths, inspiring new ideas, and guiding us towards a more authentic and fulfilling life.

The evolution of our intuition is not a linear process. It is marked by periods of rapid growth, plateaus, and even setbacks. Sometimes, our intuition may seem dormant or inaccessible, while at other times, it may surge forth with unexpected force. These fluctuations are a natural part of the process, reflecting the ebb and flow of our energy, emotions, and experiences.

Several factors can influence the development of our intuition. Our upbringing, cultural background, and personal beliefs can all shape our relationship with intuition and our willingness to trust its guidance. Our life experiences, both positive and negative, can also contribute to our intuitive development. Traumatic events, for example, can sometimes trigger a heightened sense of intuition, as we become more attuned to subtle cues and warning signs.

Our level of self-awareness also plays a crucial role in our intuitive evolution. The more we understand our own thoughts, emotions, and motivations, the easier it becomes to discern the subtle whispers of our intuition from the noise of our minds. Practices such as meditation, journaling, and therapy can help us to cultivate self-awareness and deepen our connection to our inner wisdom.

Our relationships with others can also influence our intuitive development. By surrounding ourselves with supportive and like-minded individuals who value intuition, we can create a safe and nurturing environment for our intuitive abilities to flourish. We can also learn from the experiences of others, gaining insights and wisdom that we might not have discovered on our own.

The journey of intuitive evolution is a lifelong adventure, filled with surprises, challenges, and rewards. By embracing our intuition as a valuable guide, we can navigate life's complexities with greater ease and grace, make choices that align with our deepest values, and cultivate a more meaningful and fulfilling existence. As we continue to learn, grow, and evolve, our intuition will evolve alongside us, offering us ever-deeper insights, wisdom, and guidance on our path.

ᕯᕯᕯ

Intuition is not a destination but a journey, a lifelong exploration of your innermost self. Embrace the adventure with curiosity and openness, and you will be richly rewarded.

TWENTY

Your Unique Compass: Embracing the Personal Nature of Your Intuitive Guidance

Your intuition is your compass, guiding you towards a life of purpose, fulfillment, and joy. Trust it, nurture it, and allow it to lead you home to your authentic self.

TWENTY-ONE
SUMMARY

Intuition, that elusive inner compass, is not a mystical power reserved for the select few, but a universal gift residing within each of us. It is the quiet whisper that guides us, the gut feeling that directs our choices, the unspoken knowing that illuminates our path. Cultivating and trusting this intuitive wisdom is a lifelong journey, one that involves understanding its nature, nurturing its development, and applying it in various aspects of our lives.

Our intuition is not separate from us; it is an integral part of our being, a reflection of our innermost selves. It draws upon the vast reservoir of our experiences, knowledge, and subconscious wisdom, guiding us towards choices that align with our true values and aspirations. It is a powerful ally in decision-making, helping us navigate complex situations, identify opportunities, and anticipate potential pitfalls.

The journey of cultivating intuition begins with quieting the mind and creating space for our inner wisdom to emerge. Meditation and mindfulness practices offer powerful tools for achieving this tranquility, allowing us to tune into the subtle signals of our intuition and navigate life's complexities with greater clarity and purpose. By calming the incessant chatter of our minds, we create a fertile ground for our intuition to flourish.

Nature, in its infinite wisdom, serves as a powerful mirror to our souls, reflecting our deepest emotions, desires, and fears. Spending time in nature can be a transformative experience, allowing us to reconnect with our intuition and tap into the wisdom of the natural world. The quietude of a forest, the vastness of the ocean, or the gentle breeze on our skin can awaken a sense of awe and wonder, opening our hearts and minds to the intuitive guidance that surrounds us.

Creative expression, whether through art, music, or writing, can also unlock our intuition. By engaging in these creative endeavors, we create space for our intuition to flow, revealing hidden truths, sparking new ideas, and guiding us towards a more authentic and fulfilling life. As we create, we tap into our subconscious mind, accessing a wealth of emotions, memories, and experiences that may be hidden from our conscious awareness.

Our dreams, those enigmatic nocturnal narratives, are another rich source of intuitive wisdom. By learning to interpret the symbolism and messages embedded within our dreams, we can gain valuable insights into our subconscious minds, uncover hidden desires and fears, and receive guidance on our life path.

Documenting our intuitive insights in a journal can help us to track their evolution, deepen our connection to our inner wisdom, and gain confidence in our ability to discern truth from falsehood. By reflecting on our intuitive experiences, we can identify patterns, themes, and recurring symbols, leading to a deeper understanding of ourselves and the world around us.

Applying intuition in our daily lives can transform our relationships, career choices, and overall well-being. In relationships, intuition can guide us towards deeper connections, help us navigate conflicts, and foster greater intimacy. In our careers, it can lead us to work that resonates with our inner purpose, ignites our passions, and allows us to make a meaningful contribution to the world.

In times of crisis, when the world around us seems to be crumbling, our intuition can serve as a steadfast compass, guiding us through the turbulent seas towards calmer waters. It can help us prioritize our needs, identify potential dangers and opportunities, and offer comfort and solace in the face of adversity.

The journey of cultivating intuition is not without its challenges. We may encounter various obstacles, such as overthinking, fear, negative self-talk, stress, and external influences. However, by identifying and overcoming these intuition blocks, we can reclaim our innate capacity for insight and make more aligned choices in life.

Connecting with others who value intuitive guidance can provide invaluable support and inspiration on our journey. By sharing our experiences, insights, and challenges with a community of like-minded individuals, we can deepen our understanding of intuition, gain new perspectives, and foster a sense of belonging and connection.

The development of our intuition is an ongoing process, marked by gradual shifts, sudden leaps, and profound transformations. By embracing this journey with curiosity, openness, and trust, we can tap into the infinite wisdom that resides within us, unlocking our full potential and living a life that is both meaningful and fulfilling.

ppp

Citation And References

This book represents the culmination of extensive research and meticulous analysis, incorporating a diverse range of sources, including numerous books, scholarly studies, and personal experiences. Additionally, I have scoured various websites to gather relevant information and data essential for the compilation of this work. I have taken every precaution to ensure the accuracy of the information presented and have diligently cited all sources to acknowledge their contributions.

Despite these efforts, the possibility of inadvertent errors remains. I deeply value the insights of my readers and appreciate any feedback that can help identify and rectify such inaccuracies. I encourage you to bring any discrepancies to my attention.

Your feedback is not only welcome but crucial, as it will aid in correcting current editions and enhancing the content of future ones. I am committed to maintaining the highest standards of accuracy and reliability in my work and thank you for your support and understanding.

Additionally, I firmly uphold the principle of freedom of speech and expression as guaranteed under Article 19(1)(a) of the Constitution of India, and I respect the diverse viewpoints and expressions of all readers.

❧❧❧

Other Books Of The Author

1. Empowering Minds: A Journey into Women's Self-Discovery and Power
2. The Dynamics of Motivation: Catalyzing Thought into Action
3. Meditation and Mental Well Being: The Path to Inner Peace and Clarity
4. The Psychology of Child Education: Nurturing Future Generations
5. Ethical Enlightenment: A Modern Guide to Living with Integrity
6. Voices of Empowerment: Stories of Women Rising Against Odds
7. Social Psychology in Everyday Life: Understanding Human Connections
8. The Essence of Motivational Speaking: Inspiring Change in Others
9. Balancing Acts: Women, Work, and the Will to Lead
10. Guiding with Grace: Raising Children with Compassion and Awareness
11. The Power of Positive Aging: Embracing Life After Fifty
12. Building Resilient Communities: Social Work in Action
13. The Ethical Educator: Principles for Teaching and Learning
14. From Insight to Impact: Social Psychology for a Better World
15. The Ethics of Empathy: A Guide to Ethical Living
16. The Science of Empowering the Self: Navigating Life's Challenges with Psychological Wisdom
17. The Mindful Conscious Leader: Meditation Techniques for Modern Management
18. Pioneering Spirit: Women's Pathways to Leadership and Empowerment
19. Feeling to Healing: The Role of Emotional Intelligence in Child Development
20. Transformative Talks and Words of Inspiration: Insights into Motivational Oratory

21. Green Ethics: A Path to Sustainable Living
22. Spiritual Integrity: Navigating Life with Moral Compassion
23. Clean Living, Clean Society: The Ethics of Cleanliness
24. Patriotic Spirits: Building a Nation on Positive Attitudes
25. Innovative Integrity & Vibrant Visions: The Ethical and Entrepreneurial Spirit of Gujarat
26. Youthful Visions, Endless Possibilities: Inspiring Ethics and Motivation in Children
27. Living Your Legacy: How to Motivate Others by Living Your Values
28. Secret of Healing Conversations: Ethical Practices in Counselling and Therapy
29. Creative Kindness: Crafting a Life of Compassion and Creativity
30. The Power of Appreciation: How Gratitude Can Transform Your Relationships
31. Bhagavad-Gita: Messages
32. Science of Art: The New Frontier of Fashion Modernism
33. Vivekananda's Virtues: A Blueprint for Modern Living
34. Empower Her: Navigating the Path to Women's Entrepreneurship
35. The Boundless Classroom: Innovations in Global Education
36. The Language of Leadership: Communicating with Authenticity and Impact
37. The Warrior's Mantra: Deciphering the Hanuman Chalisa
38. Echoes of Empathy: Transformative Stories of Social Service
39. Artful Living: Cultivating Creativity in Your Daily Routine
40. Finding Your Why: Discovering Your Passions and Charting Your Course
41. The Role of Social Media in Shaping Self-Esteem and Interpersonal Relationships among Adolescents
42. Karma's Tapestry: Weaving a Life of Selfless Service
43. Altruistic Alchemy: Transforming Lives Through Giving
44. The Blueprint of Pro-Activeness and Productivity: Crafting Habits for Success
45. The Simplicity with Grounded Wisdom: Embracing Authenticity

in a Complex World

46. Secret of Solopreneur's Odyssey: Navigating the Path to Self-Employment
47. Exploring Tapestry of Peace: Global Perspectives on Harmony
48. The Art and Actions of Connection: Mastering Communication for Impact
49. She Governs and at the Helm: Strategies for Political Empowerment
50. Rising Above and Rising with Grace: A Woman's Roadmap to Career Mastery
51. The Effect of Networking & Connectedness: Building Strategic Alliances for Women
52. Beyond his Barriers: Women Thriving in Male-Dominated Fields
53. Secret of Inner Compass: Navigating Life with Intuition
54. Creative & Pro-Active Muses: A Celebration of Women in the Arts
55. Unburdened: The Art of Releasing the Past
56. Amplified Voices: Speeches of Women that Astonished the World
57. Secret of Manifesting Dreams: A Woman's Guide to Intentional Living
58. Ethics and Value Based Education: Reimagining Japan's School System
59. The Moral Compass Curriculum: A Holistic Approach
60. Tech with Heart: Integrating Ethics into Digital Learning
61. Honoring Virtue: Recognizing Ethical Excellence in Education
62. Raising Good Humans: A Guide to Character Development
63. The Spark Within: Nurturing Creativity in Children
64. The Teenager Whisperer: Navigating Adolescence with Grace
65. Igniting a Passion for Learning: Inspiring Lifelong Curiosity
66. The Habit Lab: Cultivating Positive Behaviors in Children
67. Seeds of Empathy: Fostering Compassion in Young Hearts
68. The Reading Revolution: Inspiring a Love of Books in Children
69. The Learning Brain: Unlocking the Secrets of Student Success
70. Teaching for All: Differentiated Instruction Strategies
71. The Time Alchemist: Mastering Time Management for Peak Performance

72. The Resilience Factor: Transforming Setbacks into Stepping Stones
73. The Healing Touch of Nature: An Introduction to Naturopathy
74. Echoes of the Past: Healing Through Past Life Regression
75. The Spiritual Healer's Handbook: Exploring Energy Medicine
76. Crystal Clarity: Unveiling the Power of Gemstones
77. The Dream Weaver's Guide: Decoding the Language of Dreams
78. Emotional Alchemy: Transforming Pain into Power
79. Sonic Serenity: Harnessing Sound for Stress Relief
80. The Entrepreneur's Playbook: Launching Your Business with Confidence
81. Productivity Unleashed: Time Management Strategies for Entrepreneurs
82. The Problem Solver's Toolkit: Creative Solutions for Business Challenges
83. The Future is Now: Emerging Trends in Business
84. The Curious Explorer: A Child's Guide to Scientific Discovery
85. Digital Pioneers: Empowering Kids in the Tech World
86. The Young Philosopher's Guide: Exploring Life's Big Questions
87. Finding Your Voice: Communication Skills for Confident Kids
88. Nature's Playground: A Child's Guide to Outdoor Adventure
89. Growing a Greener Tomorrow: A Guide to Tree Planting & Conservation
90. Driving with Purpose: Ethical Choices on the Road
91. The Healing Touch: Cultivating Compassion in Healthcare
92. Navigating the Digital Landscape: Ethics in the Age of Social Media
93. The Ethical Closet: A Guide to Sustainable Fashion
94. The Mindful Voyager: Sustainable Travel Practices
95. The Feminine Divine: Honoring the Goddesses of India
96. Sacred Sounds: Chanting Your Way to Inner Peace
97. The Yoga Path: Uniting with the Divine Within
98. Rites of Passage: Creating Meaningful Ceremonies
99. The Chakra System: A Map of Inner Transformation
100. Spiritual Sangha: Finding Community through Satsang and

Bhajan

101. Pilgrimage of the Soul: Spiritual Journeys in India

❧❧❧

Contact

Dr. Minakshi Bansal
Social Activist
Ahmedabad, Gujarat, Bharat
minakshiindiag20@yahoo.com

❧❧❧

|| LOKAHA SAMASTHAHA SUKHINO BHAVANTU ||